W9-ABC-682

# CONTENTS

# About the Authors

It is natural that Chef Jorgé Bruce and Catering Specialist Janet Singleton have combined their talents to produce this exciting new cookbook; both have had a lifelong interest in preparing and sharing wonderful food.

As a boy, Chef Jorgé was assigned the duty of cooking dinner for his large family. While growing up as the "family chef," Chef Jorgé acquired his flair for creating good home cooked meals. Chef Jorgé refined his gourmet cooking background at the Epicurean School of Culinary Arts. He currently enjoys creating package recipes, and doing television appearances for products which are healthy and time-saving for the at-home cook.

Janet Singleton has been a chef and restaurateur since 1979. Currently, she is a sought after lecturer on home cooking and has conducted classes throughout Southern California. She caters to private clients and physicians in the Los Angeles area.

Many of the slow cooker recipes they have created use Crockery Gourmet™ as the basis for enhancing the flavors of those recipes. They believe it's the easiest way the at-home cook can create one-step tasty meals.

# NUTRITIONAL DISCLAIMER

We are not medical doctors and we are not registered dietitians. Therefore, neither the publisher, editors or authors can or will make recommendations about what you should or should not eat. We used a master cook computer program that is designed to calculate the nutritional values of foods in our recipes based upon the most recent available data from the United States Department of Agriculture

The nutritional values in food may vary substantially, depending upon such variables as geography, soil content, seasons, ripeness, processing, genetics, and method of preparation. Moreover, in some instances a nutrient value for a given foodstuff may be undetermined.

For these reasons and others, i.e., human error, please use the recipe nutritional profiles as approximate guides to the nutrient content of the recipes in this book. Those persons on special diets for the treatment of disease may require more specific nutrient data and should consult their personal physicians, registered dietitians and/or food manufacturers.

-Inland Ad News

# CROCKERY COOKING

Electric slow-cooking is perfect for today's busy at-home chef. Delicious and wholesome meals can be prepared quickly, and are ready to eat when you are! The recipes in this book have been adapted to accommodate the specific requirements of the electric slow-cooker. Each recipe has been tested and approved by the authors.

The authors of this book have selected Crockery Gourmet™ as the basis for flavor in these recipes. Crockery Gourmet™ seasoning makes crockery cooking easy, healthful, and appealing to the most discriminating tastes. The selected seasonings in Crockery Gourmet™ bring out the flavor in meats, vegetables, and poultry.

Crockery Gourmet™ comes in three flavors: Beef, Pork, and Chicken. Please note that each variety was designed to enhance the flavor of the specific meat, but does not actually contain any meat. The spices and herbs used in Crockery Gourmet™ have been combined to complement your choice of meat, poultry, or vegetables.

The recipes in this book are suitable for most electric slow cookers. Please refer to your slow cooker manual for specific information on how to operate your particular appliance.

Crockery cooking isn't limited to the cold winter months; since electric cookers do not emit heat like ovens do, it is a perfect cooking method for year-round cooking. Electric cookers are as appropriate for stews and roasts as they are for light vegetable dishes.

# CROCKERY COOKING
## WITHOUT A SLOW COOKER

The recipes herein are specially designed for use with an electric slow cooker. However, the same delicious results can also be achieved by using a Dutch oven, roaster, or earthenware casserole with a tight fitting lid. As with electric slow cookers, this cooking process allows juices from the foods and stock to condense on the lid of the pot thereby basting the food as it cooks.

To adapt the recipes for oven cooking, simply place the ingredients in a roasting pan with a lid rather than in an electric slow cooker. Make sure that the lid fits snugly, then place the food in an oven preheated to about 300 degrees. While cooking, the food should be kept at a very low simmer. Doneness times may vary from those in the recipes; check food at half the doneness time indicated. For example, if the recipe states the food will be finished in four hours, check for doneness at two hours.

To adapt the recipes for stove-top cooking, place the ingredients in a dutch oven. Cook over a low heat, stirring the sauce up from the bottom every half hour to prevent burning. The food will cook in about half the time specified in these recipes.

# SUPERIOR TOUCH™

# CROCKERY GOURMET

## SEASONING MIX
## FOR CHICKEN

*Easy To Prepare Meals For Your Slow Cooker
Dutch Oven or Roaster*

# Chicken With Vegetables

*Crockery Gourmet™ for Chicken*
*2 lbs boneless, skinless chicken*
*    breast, cut into large pieces*
*3-4 medium carrots, cut into*
*    large pieces*
*3-4 ribs celery, cut into large*
*    pieces*
*1 large onion, chopped*
*Salt and freshly ground black*
*    pepper, to taste*

Place 1-1/2 cups water in slow cooker. Slowly add Crockery Gourmet™ for Chicken to water, whisking until smooth. *Product will thicken immediately.* Add chicken and stir to coat. Place the remaining ingredients (except salt and pepper) into slow cooker on top of chicken. Cook on low setting for 7-8 hours until chicken is tender and fully cooked. One-half hour before serving, gently stir all ingredients together. Salt and pepper to taste.

**For thicker gravy:** Blend 2 Tbs flour and 1 cup warm milk together and fold into chicken and vegetables last hour of cooking.

**Chicken Ala King:** Substitute 8 oz fresh or frozen peas and 4 oz halved mushrooms for the celery. Serve over rice.

**Chicken Cacciatore:** Substitute 1 28-oz can whole or diced tomatoes for the water. Substitute 1 small can sliced olives and 1 green pepper, diced for the carrots and celery. Add 1 tsp basil and 1 tsp oregano. Do not thicken with flour and milk mixture. Serve over rice or pasta.

# Chicken

*Recipes Using* CROCKERY GOURMET™
SEASONING MIX FOR CHICKEN

The following recipes feature CROCKERY GOURMET™
SEASONING MIX FOR CHICKEN. Slow cooking makes
poultry particularly succulent and tender. Crockery Gourmet
helps bring out the flavor of chicken, turkey, and other types of
poultry. In all of these recipes, place vegetables on top of the
meat and cover  to assure they are done at about
the same time as the poultry.

*1*

# *L*emon *C*hicken

Serves 6

*Crockery Gourmet™ for Chicken*
*1 whole chicken, cut into serving-*
  *size pieces*
*1 clove garlic, minced*
*1 tsp grated lemon zest*
*2 Tbs lemon juice*
*1/2 cup white wine*
*1/8 tsp freshly black ground pepper*
*Salt, to taste*

Place 1-1/2 cups water in slow cooker. Slowly add
Crockery Gourmet™ for Chicken to water, whisking until
smooth. *Product will thicken immediately.* Place the
remaining ingredients into slow cooker, stirring to coat.
Cook on low setting for 7-8 hours until chicken is tender.
Salt and additional pepper to taste. Serve with cooked
pink beans.

# *H*oney *M*ustard *C*hicken

Serves 4

*Crockery Gourmet™ for Chicken*
*4 chicken leg quarters, skinned*
*3 Tbs honey*
*2 Tbs spicy mustard*
*1/2 cup dry white wine*
*1 medium onion, thinly sliced*
*1 tsp freshly ground black pepper*

Place 2 cups water in slow cooker. Slowly add Crockery
Gourmet™ for Chicken to water, whisking until smooth.
*Product will thicken immediately.* Place the remaining
ingredients into slow cooker, stirring to coat. Cook on
low setting for 7-8 hours or on high setting 3-4 hours,
until chicken begins to fall from the bone. Serve over
buttered egg noodles or rice.

# Chicken Stew

Serves 4-6

*Crockery Gourmet™ for Chicken*
*2 lbs chicken, cut into serving-*
*size pieces*
*3 carrots, chopped*
*3 ribs celery, chopped*
*3 onions, chopped*
*1 clove garlic, minced*
*2 plum tomatoes, chopped*
*Salt and freshly ground black*
*pepper, to taste*

Place 1-1/2 cups water in slow cooker. Slowly add Crockery Gourmet™ for Chicken to water, whisking until smooth. *Product will thicken immediately.* Add the chicken and stir to coat. Place the remaining ingredients (except tomatoes, salt and pepper) into slow cooker. Cook on low setting for 7-8 hours until chicken is tender. Add tomatoes and gently stir all ingredients 1/2 hour before serving. Salt and pepper to taste.

# Apricot Chicken

Serves 4

*Crockery Gourmet™ for Chicken*
*4 boneless, skinless chicken*
*breast halves*
*1 8-oz jar apricot preserves*
*1 cup orange juice*
*1 Tbs chopped parsley*

Place 2 cups water in slow cooker. Slowly add Crockery Gourmet™ for Chicken to water, whisking until smooth. *Product will thicken immediately.* Place the remaining ingredients into slow cooker, stirring to coat. Cook on low setting for 7-8 hours or on high setting for 3-4 hours, until chicken is fork tender. Serve over rice.

# Country Rosemary Chicken

Serves 6

*Crockery Gourmet™ for Chicken*
*6 chicken thighs*
*2 rudabegas, cubed*
*2 turnips, cubed*
*2 carrots, cubed*
*1 onion, chopped*
*1 Tbs chopped rosemary*
*Salt and freshly ground black*
  *pepper, to taste*

Place 1-1/2 cups water in slow cooker. Slowly add Crockery Gourmet™ for Chicken to water, whisking until smooth. *Product will thicken immediately.* Add chicken and stir to coat. Place the remaining ingredients into slow cooker. Cook on low setting for 6-8 hours until chicken is tender. One-half hour before serving, gently stir all ingredients together. Salt and pepper to taste.

# Chicken with Olives and Capers

Serves 4

*Crockery Gourmet™ for Chicken*
*3 lbs chicken pieces*
*1 6-oz jar capers, drained*
*1 can seedless ripe olives,*
  *drained*
*1 Tbs dill weed*
*1 tsp freshly ground black pepper*

Place 2 cups water in slow cooker. Slowly add Crockery Gourmet™ for Chicken to water, whisking until smooth. *Product will thicken immediately.* Place the remaining ingredients into slow cooker, stirring to coat. Cook on low setting for 7-8 hours or on high setting 3-4 hours until chicken begins to fall from the bone. Serve with mashed potatoes or rice.

# Tomatillo Chicken

Serves 4

Crockery Gourmet™ for Chicken
4 boneless, skinless chicken
  breast halves
2 lbs tomatillos, shucked and
  chopped
2 serrano peppers, seeded and
  chopped
1 large onion, chopped
1 bunch cilantro, chopped
1 tsp white pepper

Place 2 cups water in slow cooker. Slowly add Crockery Gourmet™ for Chicken to water, whisking until smooth. *Product will thicken immediately.* Add chicken and stir to coat. Place the remaining ingredients into slow cooker. Cook on low setting for 7-8 hours, until chicken is fork tender. One-half hour before serving, gently stir all ingredients together. Serve over rice.

# Chicken Picante

Serves 4

Crockery Gourmet™ for Chicken
4 boneless, skinless chicken
  breast halves
1 medium onion, chopped
1 bunch cilantro, chopped
2 cups picante sauce

Place 2 cups water in slow cooker. Slowly add Crockery Gourmet™ for Chicken to water, whisking until smooth. *Product will thicken immediately.* Place the remaining ingredients into slow cooker, stirring to coat. Cook on low setting for 7-8 hours or on high setting 3-4 hours until chicken is fork tender. Serve with warm tortillas or rice.

# Turkey Pasta

Serves 4

*Crockery Gourmet™ for Chicken*
*1-1/2 lbs turkey breast, cubed*
*3 carrots, chopped*
*3 ribs celery, chopped*
*1 onion, chopped*
*2 cloves garlic, minced*
*Freshly ground black pepper, to*
 *taste*
*Poultry seasoning, to taste*

Place 1-1/2 cups water in slow cooker. Slowly add Crockery Gourmet™ for Chicken to water, whisking until smooth. *Product will thicken immediately.* Add the turkey and stir to coat. Place the remaining ingredients (except pepper and poultry seasoning) into slow cooker. Cook on low setting for 7 hours until turkey is tender. One-half hour before serving, gently stir all ingredients together. Add pepper and poultry seasoning to taste. Serve over your choice of pasta.

# Chicken Dijon

Serves 4

*Crockery Gourmet™ for Chicken*
*4 boneless, skinless chicken*
 *breast halves*
*1 cup dijon mustard*
*1 Tbs dried parsley*
*1 cup white wine*
*1 tsp freshly ground black pepper*

Place 2 cups water in slow cooker. Slowly add Crockery Gourmet™ for Chicken to water, whisking until smooth. *Product will thicken immediately.* Place the remaining ingredients into slow cooker, stirring to coat. Cook on low setting for 7-8 hours until chicken is fork tender. Serve with brown rice or baked potatoes.

# Potato Mushroom Soup

Serves 4

*Crockery Gourmet™ for Chicken*
*1 lb mushrooms, sliced*
*2 medium potatoes, peeled and*
    *cubed*
*1/4 tsp freshly ground black pepper*
*2 tsp Worcestershire*
*1 bay leaf*
*Juice of one lime*
*1 bunch parsley, chopped*
*1 10-oz can evaporated milk*
*1/2 cup grated gouda cheese*

Place 2 cups water in slow cooker.  Slowly add Crockery Gourmet™ for Chicken to water, whisking until smooth.  *Product will thicken immediately.*  Place the remaining ingredients (except cheese) into slow cooker, stirring to coat.  Cook on low setting for 7-8 hours or on high setting 3-4 hours until potatoes are soft.  Sprinkle with cheese and serve with crusty french bread.

# Curried Sweet Potatoes

Serves 4

*Crockery Gourmet™ for Chicken*
*2 lbs sweet potatoes, peeled and*
    *sliced*
*1 medium onion, chopped*
*1 cup apple juice*
*2 Tbs curry powder*
*1 Tbs brown sugar*

Place 2 cups water in slow cooker.  Slowly add Crockery Gourmet™ for Chicken to water, whisking until smooth.  *Product will thicken immediately.*  Place the remaining ingredients into slow cooker, stirring to coat.  Cook on low setting for 7-8 hours or on high setting 3-4 hours.

# Rosemary Chicken with Wine

Serves 4

*Crockery Gourmet™ for Chicken*
*4 boneless, skinless chicken*
*    breast halves*
*1 medium onion, chopped*
*1 rib celery, chopped*
*1 green pepper, chopped*
*2 carrots, chopped*
*1 1/2 Tbs dried or fresh rosemary*
*1 cup white wine*
*1 tsp freshly ground black pepper*

Place 2 cups water in slow cooker. Slowly add Crockery Gourmet™ for Chicken to water, whisking until smooth. *Product will thicken immediately.* Add chicken and stir to coat. Place the remaining ingredients into slow cooker. Cook on low setting for 7-8 hours or on high setting 3-4 hours until chicken is fork tender. One-half hour before serving, gently stir all ingredients together. Serve with potatoes or rice.

# Chicken and Eggplant Parmesan

Serves 6

*Crockery Gourmet™ for Chicken*
*6 skinless chicken breast halves*
*1 eggplant, cut into 3/4-inch*
*    cubes*
*2 cloves garlic, minced*
*1/2 tsp oregano*
*1 Tbs chopped italian parsley*
*1/8 tsp freshly ground black pepper*
*6 slices mozzarella cheese*
*1/2 cup grated parmesan cheese*

Place 2 cups water in slow cooker.  Slowly add Crockery Gourmet™ for Chicken to water, whisking until smooth. *Product will thicken immediately.*  Place the next six ingredients into slow cooker, stirring to coat.  Cook on low setting for 7-8 hours until chicken is tender.  To serve, place a slice of mozzarella cheese on each piece of warm chicken and sprinkle with parmesan cheese.

# Chicken Tarragon

Serves 4-6

*Crockery Gourmet™ for Chicken*
*2 lbs chicken breast halves*
*2 Tbs lemon juice*
*1/8 tsp freshly ground black pepper*
*3 carrots, chopped*
*3 ribs celery, chopped*
*4 potatoes, quartered*
*1 large onion, chopped*
*2 Tbs freshly chopped tarragon*

Place 2 cups water in slow cooker. Slowly add Crockery Gourmet™ for Chicken to water, whisking until smooth. *Product will thicken immediately.* Add chicken, lemon juice and pepper and stir to coat. Place the remaining ingredients into slow cooker. Cook on low setting for 6-8 hours until chicken is cooked through and tender. One-half hour before serving, gently stir all ingredients together.

# Chicken and Tomatoes

Serves 6

*Crockery Gourmet™ for Chicken*
*2-3 lbs chicken, cut into servings*
*1 6-oz can tomato paste*
*1/2 cup sherry*
*1/2 lb mushrooms, sliced*
*1/4 cup chopped italian parsley*
*12 pearl onions*
*2 fresh tomatoes, chopped*

Place 2 cups water in slow cooker. Slowly add Crockery Gourmet™ for Chicken to water, whisking until smooth. *Product will thicken immediately.* Place the next six ingredients into slow cooker, stirring to coat. Cook on low setting for 7-8 hours. Add tomatoes and cook another 30-45 minutes. Serve with rice or mashed potatoes.

# Chicken and Dumplings

*Crockery Gourmet™ for Chicken*
*3 lb chicken, cut into servings*
*2 cloves garlic, minced*
*1/2 cup white wine*
*12 pearl onions, peeled*
*1 Tbs minced italian parsley*
*1/4 tsp freshly ground black pepper*
*3 Tbs flour mixed with 1 cup*
    *water*
*1 8-oz tube biscuit dough*

Place 2 cups water in slow cooker. Slowly add Crockery Gourmet™ for Chicken to water, whisking until smooth. *Product will thicken immediately.* Place the next six ingredients into slow cooker, stirring to coat. Cook on low setting for 7-8 hours until chicken is tender.

Turn the slow cooker to high setting. Stir in flour and water mixture to desired thickness. Cut each biscuit into quarters and place them over the chicken. Cook on high setting another 30 minutes until biscuits are cooked.

# 𝒯urkey 𝔅reast

Serves 6

*Crockery Gourmet™ for Chicken*
*3 lbs turkey breast, skinned*
*1 clove garlic, minced*
*1 small onion, diced*
*1 carrot, diced*
*2 ribs celery, diced*
*4 new potatoes, halved*
*2 Tbs minced italian parsley*
*1/2 tsp poultry seasoning*
*1/8 tsp freshly ground black pepper*

Place 2 cups water in slow cooker. Slowly add Crockery Gourmet™ for Chicken to water, whisking until smooth. *Product will thicken immediately.* Add turkey and stir to coat. Place the remaining ingredients into slow cooker. Cook on low setting for 7-8 hours until turkey is cooked through. One-half hour before serving, gently stir all ingredients together.

# 𝒞hicken 𝒮atay

Serves 4

*Crockery Gourmet™ for Chicken*
*4 boneless, skinless chicken*
        *breast halves*
*1 bunch cilantro, chopped*
*3/4 cup sugar*
*1 tsp freshly ground black pepper*
*1 cup creamy peanut butter*

Place 2 cups water in slow cooker. Slowly add Crockery Gourmet™ for Chicken to water, whisking until smooth. *Product will thicken immediately.* Place the remaining ingredients into slow cooker, stirring to coat. Cook on low setting for 7-8 hours, stirring once, until chicken is cooked through. Serve with white rice.

# ℐambalaya Shrimp

*Crockery Gourmet™ for Chicken*
*2 tsp Louisiana hot sauce*
*2-1/2 lb chicken, cut into serving-*
    *size pieces*
*2 cloves garlic, minced*
*1/2 tsp oregano*
*1/2 tsp basil*
*1/8 tsp freshly ground black pepper*
*2 onions, chopped*
*1 carrots, sliced into medallions*
*1 14-oz can chopped tomatoes*
*1 lb raw medium shrimp, shelled*
    *and deveined*
*2 cups cooked rice or 1-lb bag of*
    *quick-cooking rice*

Place 2 cups water and hot sauce in slow cooker. Slowly add Crockery Gourmet™ for Chicken to water, whisking until smooth. *Product will thicken immediately.* Add chicken, garlic, oregano, basil and pepper and stir to coat. Place the onions, carrots and tomatoes into slow cooker. Cook on low setting for 6-7 hours. Turn the slow cooker up to high setting and stir in shrimp and rice. Cook another 30-40 minutes until shrimp and rice are cooked through.

# Stuffed Chicken with Carrots

Serves 6

*1 16-oz pkg stove top-type dressing*
*1/2 tsp minced rosemary*
*Crockery Gourmet™ for Chicken*
*1/4 cup white wine*
*1 4-lb chicken*
*Freshly ground black pepper*
*1 lb baby carrots*
*2 Tbs flour dissolved in 2 Tbs*
*    milk*

Prepare dressing in accordance with package directions, adding rosemary. Place 1-1/4 cups water and wine in slow cooker. Slowly add Crockery Gourmet™ for Chicken to water, whisking until smooth. *Product will thicken immediately.* Stuff the chicken with prepared dressing and truss for easy removal from slow cooker. Place the carrots into slow cooker, stirring to coat. Place the chicken on top of the carrots and sprinkle with pepper and additional minced rosemary. Cook on low setting for 7-8 hours until chicken is fork tender and cooked through. Add flour mixture to thicken sauce if desired. Remove chicken and carve; serve with stuffing and carrots.

**Note:** For a browner chicken, place chicken in a 400° oven for 15 minutes prior to slow cooking.

# 𝒯urkey 𝒮trip 𝒞hop 𝒮uey

Serves 6

*Crockery Gourmet™ for Chicken*
*1 tsp Better Than Bouillon™*
    *Chicken Base or concentrated*
    *chicken stock*
*2 lbs turkey breast, cut into strips*
*1 tsp minced crystallized ginger*
*1 cup sliced celery*
*1 6-oz can water chestnuts,*
    *drained and sliced*
*1 onion, sliced*
*2 Tbs soy sauce*
*1 cup sliced mushrooms*
*3/4 lb bean sprouts*
*Slivered almonds*

Place 2 cups water in slow cooker. Slowly add Crockery Gourmet™ for Chicken and concentrated stock to water, whisking until smooth. *Product will thicken immediately.* Place the remaining ingredients (except almonds) into slow cooker, stirring to coat. Cook on low setting for 5-6 hours until chicken is cooked through. Sprinkle with almonds and serve with white rice.

# Southern Corn Chowder

Serves 4

*4-5 slices bacon*
*Crockery Gourmet™ for Chicken*
*1/4 cup bacon drippings*
*2 onions, chopped*
*2 cups diced potatoes*
*1/2 cup chopped celery*
*2 bay leaves*
*1 10-oz can evaporated milk*
*2 16-oz cans cream style corn*
*1 bunch cilantro, chopped*
*1/2 tsp freshly ground black pepper*

Cook bacon until very crisp. Reserve drippings. Crumble bacon and save for garnish. Place 2 cups water in slow cooker. Slowly add Crockery Gourmet™ for Chicken to water, whisking until smooth. *Product will thicken immediately.* Place the remaining ingredients into slow cooker, stirring to coat. Cook on low setting for 3-4 hours. Serve as a main course or heavy first course, sprinkled with reserved bacon bits.

# *C*hicken *J*ambalaya

Serves 4

*Crockery Gourmet™ for Chicken*
*4 boneless, skinless chicken*
*    breast halves, cubed*
*3 Tbs bacon drippings*
*1 medium onion, chopped*
*1/2 cup chopped celery*
*1/2 cup chopped green pepper*
*1-lb can chopped tomatoes with*
*    liquid*
*4 tsp worcestershire*
*4 cups cooked rice*

Place 2 cups water in slow cooker. Slowly add Crockery Gourmet™ for Chicken to water, whisking until smooth. *Product will thicken immediately.* Add chicken and bacon drippings and stir to coat. Place the remaining ingredients (except rice) into slow cooker. Cook on low setting for 5-6 hours or on high setting 3-4 hours until chicken is cooked through and tender. One-half hour before serving, gently stir all ingredients together. Serve on rice or stir rice into jambalaya before serving.

# Chicken Tetrazzini

Serves 4

*Crockery Gourmet™ for Chicken*
*4 boneless, skinless chicken*
    *breast halves, cubed*
*2 cloves garlic, minced*
*2 8-oz cans mushroom soup*
*4 ribs celery, chopped*
*1/4 cup chopped green pepper*
*1/4 cup chopped onion*
*1 cup stewed tomatoes*
*4 cups cooked egg noodles*
*1 cup shredded sharp cheddar*
    *cheese*

Place 2 cups water in slow cooker. Slowly add Crockery Gourmet™ for Chicken to water, whisking until smooth. *Product will thicken immediately.* Add chicken, garlic and mushroom soup and stir to coat. Place the remaining ingredients (except noodles and cheese) into slow cooker. Cook on low setting for 4-5 hours or on high setting 3-4 hours until chicken is cooked through and tender. One-half hour before serving, gently stir all ingredients together. Serve over noodles and sprinkle with cheese.

# Bok Choy Chicken

*Crockery Gourmet™ for Chicken*
*4 boneless, skinless chicken*
    *breast halves*
*1 medium onion, chopped*
*2 serrano peppers, seeded and*
    *chopped*
*1 cup lime juice*
*1 bunch cilantro, chopped*
*1 4-oz can water chestnuts,*
    *drained and sliced*
*2 bunches bok choy, chopped*

Place 2 cups water in slow cooker. Slowly add Crockery Gourmet™ for Chicken to water, whisking until smooth. *Product will thicken immediately.* Place the remaining ingredients (except boy choy) into slow cooker, stirring to coat. Cook on low setting for 7-8 hours or on high setting 3-4 hours until chicken is fork tender. Add bok choy for the last 1/2-hour of cooking. Serve over rice.

***To serve as a stew:*** Cut the chicken into bite-sized pieces and cook as above.

# Chicken with Sweet Red Peppers

Serves 4-6

*Crockery Gourmet™ for Chicken*
*4 chicken breast halves*
*3 cloves garlic, minced*
*1/8 tsp freshly ground black pepper*
*1/2 cup white wine*
*6 large sweet red peppers, roasted,*
*    peeled and cut into strips*
*    (prepared peppers may be*
*    used)*

Place 2 cups water in slow cooker. Slowly add Crockery Gourmet™ for Chicken to water, whisking until smooth. *Product will thicken immediately.* Add chicken, garlic, pepper and wine and stir to coat. Place the peppers into slow cooker. Cook on low setting for 6-8 hours until chicken is cooked through and tender. Serve with rice, arranging chicken with peppers on top.

# Chicken Creole

Serves 4-6

*Crockery Gourmet™ for Chicken*
*2 lb chicken, cut into servings*
*1 green pepper, chopped*
*1 bunch green onions, chopped*
*1 6-oz can tomato paste*
*1 16-oz can chopped tomatoes*
*1/4 lb cooked ham, cubed*
*1/4-1/2 tsp tabasco sauce*
*1/2 lb smoked sausage, cubed*

Place 2 cups water in slow cooker. Slowly add Crockery Gourmet™ for Chicken to water, whisking until smooth. *Product will thicken immediately.* Place the remaining ingredients into slow cooker, stirring to coat. Cook on low setting for 7-8 hours until chicken is cooked through. Serve with rice.

# Notes

# Notes

# Notes

# SUPERIOR TOUCH™

# CROCKERY GOURMET

## SEASONING MIX
## FOR BEEF

*Easy To Prepare Meals For Your Slow Cooker*
*Dutch Oven or Roaster*

# Beef Stew

*Crockery Gourmet™ for Beef*
*2-3 lbs stewing beef, cut into*
*large pieces, trimmed*
*2 large carrots, chopped*
*3 ribs celery, chopped*
*2 potatoes, quartered*
*1 onion, chopped*
*Salt and freshly ground black*
*pepper, to taste*
*Cooked rice or bread*

Place 2 cups water in slow cooker. Slowly add Crockery Gourmet™ for Beef to water, whisking until smooth. *Product will thicken immediately.* Add beef and stir to coat. Place the remaining ingredients (except salt, pepper and rice or bread) into slow cooker on top of beef. Cook on low setting for 8-9 hours until beef is tender. One-half hour before serving, gently stir all ingredients together. Salt and pepper to taste. Serve over rice or with bread.

**Beef Burgundy:** Substitute 1 cup burgundy wine and 1 cup water for the 2 cups water. Substitute 8 oz fresh mushrooms, halved for carrots, celery and potatoes. Serve over rice or noodles.

**Beef Stroganoff:** Substitute 8 oz fresh mushrooms, halved for carrots, celery and potatoes. After cooking, just before serving, stir in 8 oz sour cream. Serve over noodles.

# Beef

*Recipes Using* CROCKERY GOURMET™
SEASONING MIX FOR BEEF

The following recipes feature CROCKERY GOURMET™
SEASONING MIX FOR BEEF. Slow-cooking is perfectly suit-
ed for almost all cuts of beef. Slow-cooking can make even
the less-tender cuts tender and delicious. It is not necessary to
brown meat before you cook. When the recipe calls for
vegetables, cut them into small-to-medium-sized pieces and
place them on top of the meat, covering to assure
thorough cooking.

# 7urnip Beef Stew

Serves 6

Crockery Gourmet™ for Beef
2-1/2 lbs stewing beef, cut into
   large pieces, trimmed
2 carrots, chopped
1 onion, chopped
2 cloves garlic, minced
2 potatoes, cut into 1/4-inch
   slices
2 turnips, cut into 1/4-inch slices
1 green pepper, chopped
Salt and freshly ground black
   pepper, to taste

Place 1-1/2 cups water in slow cooker. Slowly add Crockery Gourmet™ for Beef to water, whisking until smooth. *Product will thicken immediately.* Add beef and stir to coat. Place the remaining ingredients into slow cooker. Cook on low setting for 7 hours until beef is tender. One-half hour before serving, gently stir all ingredients together. Salt and pepper to taste.

# Beefy Beans and Rice

Serves 4

Crockery Gourmet™ for Beef
1 8-oz can pinto beans with liquid
1 8-oz can black beans with liquid
1 8-oz can corn, drained
1 8-oz can mushrooms, stems
   and pieces, drained
1 bunch green onion, sliced

Place 1-1/2 cups water in slow cooker. Slowly add Crockery Gourmet™ for Beef to water, whisking until smooth. *Product will thicken immediately.* Place the remaining ingredients into slow cooker, stirring to coat. Cook on low setting for 5-6 hours.

# 7angy Beef Short Ribs

Serves 4

*Crockery Gourmet™ for Beef*
*3 lbs beef short ribs*
*1 medium onion, chopped*
*1 clove garlic, minced*
*2 ribs celery, chopped*
*2 Tbs brown sugar*
*1 Tbs worcestershire*
*2 Tbs catsup*
*1 cup sherry*
*1 Tbs Better Than Bouillon™*
   *Chili Base*

Place 2 cups water in slow cooker. Slowly add Crockery Gourmet™ for Beef to water, whisking until smooth. *Product will thicken immediately.* Place the remaining ingredients into slow cooker, stirring to coat. Cook on low setting for 8-9 hours or on high setting for 4-5 hours until beef is tender. Serve with baked potato or rice.

# Beefy Barley Soup

Serves 4

*Crockery Gourmet™ for Beef*
*1 lb stew beef, cubed*
*1 lb pearl barley*
*1 medium onion, chopped*
*2 cloves garlic, minced*
*1 Tbs freshly ground black pepper*

Place 2 cups water in slow cooker. Slowly add Crockery Gourmet™ for Beef to water, whisking until smooth. *Product will thicken immediately.* Stir in an additional 3 cups water and place the remaining ingredients into slow cooker, stirring to coat. Cook on low setting for 5-6 hours until barley is tender.

# West Indies Stew

*Crockery Gourmet™ for Beef*
*3 lbs  combination lean beef and*
*    pork, cut into large pieces*
*2 carrots, chopped*
*2 ribs celery, chopped*
*1 green/yellow plantain, cut into*
*    1/4-inch slices, then halved*
*1 ear corn, cut into 1-inch disks,*
*    then quartered*
*1 turnip, cut into large pieces*
*1 sweet potato or yam, cut into*
*    large pieces*
*1 white or russet potato, cut into*
*    large pieces*
*1/2 cup chopped cilantro*
*1 clove garlic, minced*
*1 tomato, seeded and chopped*
*1 green pepper, chopped*
*1 onion, chopped*
*1 tsp Better Than Bouillon™ Ham*
*    Base*
*Freshly ground black pepper*

Place 1-1/2 cups water in slow cooker. Slowly add Crockery Gourmet™ for Beef to water, whisking until smooth. *Product will thicken immediately.* Add beef and pork and stir to coat. Place the next seven ingredients into slow cooker. In a separate bowl, combine cilantro, garlic, tomato, green pepper and onion. Spread cilantro mixture over meat and vegetables in the slow cooker. Cook on low setting for 6-8 hours until beef, pork and vegetables are tender. One-half hour before serving, gently stir all ingredients together and add Better Than Bouillon™ Ham Base and pepper to taste.

# Beef Tips with Onions and Port

Serves 4-6

*Crockery Gourmet™ for Beef*
*2 lbs beef tips cut into small*
*    pieces*
*2 bay leaves*
*1 tsp freshly ground black pepper*
*1 clove garlic, minced*
*1 cup port*
*1 Tbs dried oregano*
*12 boiling onions, peeled*
*2 carrots, sliced*
*Cooked rice*

Place 2 cups water in slow cooker. Slowly add Crockery Gourmet™ for Beef to water, whisking until smooth. *Product will thicken immediately.* Add all ingredients except onions, carrots and rice and stir to coat. Place the onions and carrots on top of the beef. Cook on low setting for 8-9 hours or on high setting for 4-5 hours until beef is tender. One-half hour before serving, gently stir all ingredients together. Serve over white rice.

# Corned Beef and Cabbage

Serves 4

*Crockery Gourmet™ for Beef*
*2 lb corned beef brisket with*
*    spices and liquid*
*1 lb cabbage, chopped in large*
*    pieces*

Place 2 cups water in slow cooker. Slowly add Crockery Gourmet™ for Beef to water, whisking until smooth. *Product will thicken immediately.* Stir in an additional 2 cups water and place the beef brisket into slow cooker, submerging. Cook on low setting for 6-7 hours. Add cabbage and cook one more hour.

# *My Oh My M*eatballs

Serves 4-6

1-1/2 lbs ground beef, pork, or
    combination
1 egg, slightly beaten
1 tsp italian seasonings (oregano,
    thyme, basil)
2 cloves garlic, minced
1/2 cup seasoned dried bread
    crumbs
1 tsp worcestershire
1/4 cup finely diced onion
1/4 cup finely diced green pepper
1 tsp freshly ground black pepper

Crockery Gourmet™ for Beef
1 16-oz can chopped tomatoes
1 Tbs sugar
1 Tbs oregano
2 cloves garlic
Cooked spaghetti or tube-shaped
    pasta

In a bowl, combine first nine ingredients. Form into
1-1/2-inch balls. Set aside.

Place 2 cups water in slow cooker. Slowly add Crockery
Gourmet™ for Beef to water, whisking until smooth.
*Product will thicken immediately.* Place the remaining
ingredients (except pasta) into slow cooker, stirring to
coat. Gently place formed meatballs into sauce. Cook
on low setting for 7-8 hours or on high setting for 3-4
hours. Serve over hot spaghetti or tube pasta.

# $\mathcal{M}$ushroom and $\mathcal{P}$otato $\mathcal{S}$oup

Serves 4

*Crockery Gourmet™ for Beef*
*2 lbs mushrooms, sliced*
*2 onions, sliced*
*2 lbs new potatoes, cubed with*
*    skins on*
*1 Tbs Better Than Bouillon™ Beef*
*    Base or concentrated beef*
*    stock*
*1 cup sherry*
*2 tsp tarragon*
*2 tsp freshly ground black pepper*
*Biscuits or rolls*

Place 3 cups water in slow cooker. Slowly add Crockery Gourmet™ for Beef to water, whisking until smooth. *Product will thicken immediately.* Place the remaining ingredients (except biscuits or rolls) into slow cooker, stirring to coat. Cook on low setting for 7-8 hours or on high setting for 3-4 hours. Serve with biscuits or rolls.

# $\mathcal{T}$eriyaki $\mathcal{B}$eef

Serves 4

*Crockery Gourmet™ for Beef*
*2 lbs chuck steak, thinly sliced*
*1 tsp ginger*
*1 tsp sugar*
*2 cloves garlic, minced*
*1/4 cup soy sauce*
*Cooked white rice*

Place 2 cups water in slow cooker. Slowly add Crockery Gourmet™ for Beef to water, whisking until smooth. *Product will thicken immediately.* Place the remaining ingredients (except rice) into slow cooker, stirring to coat. Cook on low setting for 7-8 hours until beef is tender. Serve with hot rice.

# Castiglioni Stew

Serves 4

*Crockery Gourmet™ for Beef*
*1 lb lean stew meat, cubed*
*1 6-oz can tomato sauce*
*1 cup red wine*
*1 lb russet potatoes, cubed*
*1 onion, chopped*
*1 cup sliced carrots*
*1/2 cup chopped celery*
*1 8-oz can seedless ripe olives,*
   *drained*
*1/3 lb mushrooms, sliced*

Place 2 cups water in slow cooker. Slowly add Crockery Gourmet™ for Beef to water, whisking until smooth. *Product will thicken immediately.* Add beef, tomato sauce and wine and stir to coat. Place the remaining ingredients into slow cooker. Cook on low setting for 8-9 hours until beef is tender. One-half hour before serving, gently stir all ingredients together. Serve as a main dish with a side salad and bread.

# Pot au Feu

*Crockery Gourmet™ for Beef*
*3 lbs boneless rump roast of beef*
*1 cup red wine*
*2 cloves garlic, minced*
*2 tsp thyme*
*2 bay leaves*
*1 onion, chopped*
*2 cups baby carrots*
*2 turnips, chopped*
*2 leeks, white part only, chopped*

Place 2 cups water in slow cooker. Slowly add Crockery Gourmet™ for Beef to water, whisking until smooth. *Product will thicken immediately.* Add beef, wine, garlic, thyme and bay leaves and stir to coat. Place the vegetables into slow cooker. Cook on low setting for 8-9 hours or on high setting for 4-5 hours until beef falls apart. One-half hour before serving, gently stir all ingredients together. Serve as main dish stew with a side salad and hearty bread.

# 7asty 7ruit 7lank Steak

Serves 4

*Crockery Gourmet™ for Beef*
*1-1/2 lb flank steak*
*1 30-oz can fruit cocktail*
*1 Tbs lemon juice*
*1 tsp vinegar*
*1 clove garlic, minced*

Place 1-1/2 cups water in slow cooker. Slowly add Crockery Gourmet™ for Beef to water, whisking until smooth. *Product will thicken immediately.* Place the flank steak into slow cooker, stirring to coat. Drain the fruit cocktail into a bowl and set aside the fruit. Mix the remaining ingredients into the fruit juice and pour over the meat. Cook on low setting for 8-9 hours until beef is tender. Stir in the fruit and continue cooking another 20 minutes to warm fruit. Remove the steak and slice. Serve with fruit sauce on top.

# Barbecued Beef

Serves 6

*Crockery Gourmet™ for Beef*
*2-1/2 lbs beef stew meat*
*1/4 tsp freshly ground black pepper*
*1/2 tsp Better Than Bouillon™*
    *Beef Base (or concentrated*
    *beef stock) stirred into 1 cup*
    *smoked barbecue sauce*
*1 onion, diced*
*2 1-lb cans lima beans, drained*

Place 1-1/2 cups water in slow cooker. Slowly add Crockery Gourmet™ for Beef to water, whisking until smooth. *Product will thicken immediately.* Place the next five ingredients into slow cooker, stirring to coat. Cook on low setting for 6-7 hours until beef is tender. Add beans 1/2 hour before serving.

# Ratatouille

*Crockery Gourmet™ for Beef*
*4 Tbs olive oil*
*2 onions, sliced*
*3 cloves garlic, minced*
*1 lb eggplant, cubed*
*5 medium zucchini, sliced*
*2 red bell peppers, chopped*
*3 tsp basil*
*1 bunch parsley, chopped*
*5 large beefsteak tomatoes,*
    *chopped*
*1 cup red wine*

Place 2 cups water in slow cooker. Slowly add Crockery Gourmet™ for Beef to water, whisking until smooth. *Product will thicken immediately.* Place the remaining ingredients into slow cooker, stirring to coat. Cook on low setting for 6-7 hours or on high setting for 3-5 hours. Great warm or cold with bread or rice.

# Beef Goulash

Serves 6

*Crockery Gourmet™ for Beef*
*3 lbs boneless chuck roast, cubed*
*4 onions, chopped*
*2 cloves garlic, minced*
*1/4 cup bacon drippings*
*1 green onion, chopped*
*4 Tbs paprika*
*1 cup red wine*

Place 2 cups water in slow cooker. Slowly add Crockery Gourmet™ for Beef to water, whisking until smooth. *Product will thicken immediately.* Place the remaining ingredients into slow cooker, stirring to coat. Cook on low setting for 8-9 hours until beef falls apart.

# Southwestern Chili

*Crockery Gourmet™ for Beef*
*2 lbs lean beef, cut into small*
*pieces*
*1 large jalapeno, minced*
*1/2 tsp crushed red pepper*
*1 Tbs chopped cilantro*
*1 3-oz can tomato paste*
*2 cloves garlic, minced*
*1/2 tsp marjoram*
*1 medium onion, chopped*
*1 1-lb can pinto beans, drained*
*1 Tbs white vinegar*
*Better Than Bouillon™ Chili Base*
*and/or chili powder to taste*

Place 1-1/2 cups water in slow cooker. Slowly add Crockery Gourmet™ for Beef to water, whisking until smooth. *Product will thicken immediately.* Place the next eight ingredients into slow cooker, stirring to coat. Cook on low setting for 8-9 hours. Add beans and vinegar to meat and cook another 30 minutes. Add Better Than Bouillon™ Chili Base and/or chili powder to taste.

# Steak and Egg Noodles

*Crockery Gourmet™ for Beef*
*2 lbs boneless round steak*
*Freshly ground black pepper*
*1 tsp dill weed*
*1 onion, sliced*
*1 green pepper, julienned*
*1/4 cup flour dissolved into*
  *1/4 cup water*
*Sour cream (optional)*
*Cooked egg noodles*

Place 1-1/2 cups water in slow cooker. Slowly add Crockery Gourmet™ for Beef to water, whisking until smooth. *Product will thicken immediately.* Pepper the steak and place all but the flour/water mixture, sour cream and noodles into the slow cooker, stirring to coat. Cook on low setting for 8-9 hours until beef is tender. Remove beef and add flour/water mixture to sauce to thicken. Cook another 10 minutes. If desired, add sour cream just before serving. Serve hot over egg noodles.

# Baja Beef Strips

Serves 4-6

*Crockery Gourmet™ for Beef*
*2 lbs boneless round steak, cut*
*into strips*
*1 clove garlic, minced*
*1/4 tsp freshly ground black pepper*
*1 Tbs chili powder*
*1 onion, chopped*
*2 ortega chilies, chopped*
*1 16-oz can crushed tomatoes*
*1 16-oz can kidney or pink*
*beans, drained*
*1 tsp white vinegar*

Place 1-1/2 cups water in slow cooker. Slowly add Crockery Gourmet™ for Beef to water, whisking until smooth. *Product will thicken immediately.* Place the next seven ingredients into slow cooker, stirring to coat. Cook on low setting for 8-9 hours until beef is tender. Add beans and vinegar 30 minutes before serving. Serve over rice.

# Portobello Soup

Serves 4

*Crockery Gourmet™ for Beef*
*2 cups hearty red wine*
*2 lb portobello mushrooms, cut*
*into 1/4-inch slices*
*1 lb pearl onions, peeled*

Place 2 cups water in slow cooker. Slowly add Crockery Gourmet™ for Beef to water, whisking until smooth. *Product will thicken immediately.* Stir in wine and an additional 3 cups water. Place the remaining ingredients into slow cooker, stirring to coat. Cook on low setting for 4-5 hours until mushrooms are tender. Additional water may be added for a thinner soup.

# *New England Roast*

*Crockery Gourmet™ for Beef*
*2-3 lb beef roast*
*1 Tbs grated horseradish*
*1/8 tsp freshly ground black pepper*
*4 carrots, chopped*
*2 ribs celery, chopped*
*2 medium onions, chopped*
*2 Tbs vinegar*
*1 tsp Better Than Bouillon™ Beef*
  *or Ham Base or other*
  *concentrated stock*
*1 small cabbage, cut into wedges*
*1/4 cup flour dissolved into*
  *1/4 cup water (optional)*

Place 1-1/2 cups water in slow cooker. Slowly add Crockery Gourmet™ for Beef to water, whisking until smooth. *Product will thicken immediately.* Place the next eight ingredients into slow cooker, stirring to coat. Place cabbage on top and cook on low setting for 7-8 hours until beef is tender. Remove meat to a platter and place vegetables on top. Thicken the sauce with flour/water mixture if desired, cooking another 10-15 minutes.

# *M*eat *B*all *S*tew

Serves 4

> 2 lbs lean ground beef
> 1/2 cup italian seasoned bread
>    crumbs
> 2 eggs, slightly beaten
> 1/4 cup milk
> 1 tsp Better Than Bouillon™ Beef
>    Base
> 1/2 tsp salt
> 1/8 tsp garlic powder
> 1/4 tsp freshly ground black pepper
>
> Crockery Gourmet™ for Beef
> 2 cloves garlic, minced
> 2 carrots, chopped
> 1 green pepper, chopped
> 1 onion, chopped
> 1 16-oz can stewed tomatoes
> 1 tsp oregano
> 1 tsp basil
> 1/4 tsp freshly ground black pepper
> 2 Tbs minced italian parsley

In a bowl, combine first eight ingredients. Form into 1-1/2-inch balls. Set aside.

Place 1-1/2 cups water in slow cooker. Slowly add Crockery Gourmet™ for Beef to water, whisking until smooth. *Product will thicken immediately.* Stir in the remaining ingredients. Place the formed meatballs into the slow cooker and gently stir to coat. Cook on low setting for 6-7 hours.

# Corned Beef and Vegetables

Serves 6

*Crockery Gourmet™ for Beef*
*3 lbs corned beef (without*
*    seasoning packet)*
*2 cloves garlic, minced*
*2 carrots, chopped*
*1 large onion, chopped*
*2 potatoes, quartered*
*1 head cabbage, cut into wedges*

Place 1-1/2 cups water in slow cooker. Slowly add Crockery Gourmet™ for Beef to water, whisking until smooth. *Product will thicken immediately.* Place the next five ingredients into slow cooker, stirring to coat. Place the cabbage on top and cook on low setting for 9-10 hours until beef is tender.

# Old Ranch Beef and Beans

Serves 6

*Crockery Gourmet™ for Beef*
*1 lb lean beef, cut into small*
*    chunks*
*2 16-oz cans pork and beans*
*1 16-oz can kidney beans,*
*    drained*
*1/2 cup catsup*
*2 Tbs mustard*
*1 Tbs vinegar*
*3 green onions, minced*

Place 1-1/2 cups water in slow cooker. Slowly add Crockery Gourmet™ for Beef to water, whisking until smooth. *Product will thicken immediately.* Place the next six ingredients into slow cooker, stirring to coat. Place onions on top of mixture. Cook on low setting for 3-4 hours until beef is tender. Stir before serving.

# Vegetable Short Rib Soup

Serves 6

*Crockery Gourmet™ for Beef*
*1-1/2 lb beef short ribs*
*1 onion, chopped*
*2 ribs celery, chopped*
*2 carrots, chopped*
*2 large potatoes, peeled and diced*
*1 lb frozen sweet corn*
*1-lb can chopped tomatoes*
*2 turnips, peeled and diced*
*1 cup beef stock (optional)*

Place 2 cups water in slow cooker. Slowly add Crockery Gourmet™ for Beef to water, whisking until smooth. *Product will thicken immediately.* Place the remaining ingredients into slow cooker, stirring to coat. Cook on low setting for 8-9 hours or on high setting for 4-5 hours until beef is tender. Add beef stock if desired for a thinner soup.

# French Onion Soup

Serves 4

*Crockery Gourmet™ for Beef*
*4 onions, thinly sliced*
*1 Tbs Better Than Bouillon™ Beef*
*Base or concentrated beef*
*stock*
*1-1/2 cups red wine*
*Toasted croutons*
*1 cup shredded mozzarella cheese*

Place 2 cups water in slow cooker. Slowly add Crockery Gourmet™ for Beef to water, whisking until smooth. *Product will thicken immediately.* Place the remaining ingredients (except croutons and cheese) and another 2 cups water into slow cooker, stirring to coat. Cook on low setting for 7-8 hours. Serve with toasted croutons and shredded mozzarella cheese.

# Beef Stroganoff

Serves 4

*Crockery Gourmet™ for Beef*
*2 lbs beef stew meat*
*1 cup tomato juice*
*2 Tbs Better Than Bouillon™ Beef*
    *Base or concentrated beef*
    *stock dissolved in 2 cups*
    *warm water*
*1 large onion, chopped*
*2 lbs mushrooms*
*1 cup sour cream*

Place 2 cups water in slow cooker. Slowly add Crockery Gourmet™ for Beef to water, whisking until smooth. *Product will thicken immediately.* Add beef, tomato juice and beef stock and stir to coat. Place onion and mushrooms into slow cooker. Cook on low setting for 7-8 hours until beef is tender. One-half hour before serving, gently stir all ingredients together. Stir in sour cream just before serving.

# Dilled Pot Roast

Serves 6

*Crockery Gourmet™ for Beef*
*3 lb pot roast*
*1 Tbs vinegar*
*2 tsp fresh dill weed*
*1/8 tsp freshly ground black pepper*
*3-4 potatoes, quartered*
*3-4 carrots, cut into medallions*

Place 1-1/2 cups water in slow cooker. Slowly add Crockery Gourmet™ for Beef to water, whisking until smooth. *Product will thicken immediately.* Add beef, vinegar, dill and pepper and stir to coat. Place the vegetables into slow cooker. Cook on low setting for 8-9 hours until beef is tender. One-half hour before serving, gently stir all ingredients together.

**Richer Sauce:** Stir in 3 Tbs flour dissolved in 1/4 cup water and 1 cup sour cream.

# Irish Stew

Serves 4

*Crockery Gourmet™ for Beef*
*2 lbs lamb, cubed*
*1 bay leaf*
*1 tsp freshly ground black pepper*
*1 cup irish whiskey*
*1 large onion, sliced*
*2 lbs potatoes, peeled and sliced*

Place 2 cups water in slow cooker. Slowly add Crockery Gourmet™ for Beef to water, whisking until smooth. *Product will thicken immediately.* Add lamb, bay leaf and pepper and stir to coat. Place the remaining ingredients into slow cooker, stirring to coat. Cook on low setting for 7-8 hours or on high setting for 3-4 hours. One-half hour before serving, gently stir all ingredients together.

# Beef Short Ribs and Potatoes

Serves 6

Crockery Gourmet™ for Beef
3 lbs lean beef short ribs
2 Tbs catsup
1/4 tsp freshly ground black pepper
4 carrots, quartered
1 onion, sliced
4 potatoes, peeled and quartered

Place 1-1/2 cups water in slow cooker. Slowly add Crockery Gourmet™ for Beef to water, whisking until smooth. *Product will thicken immediately.* Add ribs, catsup and pepper and stir to coat. Place the remaining ingredients into slow cooker. Cook on low setting for 7-8 hours until beef is tender. One-half hour before serving, gently stir all ingredients together.

# Stewed Calves Liver

Serves 6

Crockery Gourmet™ for Beef
2 lbs calves liver, sliced
1 1-lb can stewed tomatoes
1 bay leaf
5 sliced bacon, cut into thirds
2 carrots, chopped
2 ribs celery, chopped
1 medium onion, chopped
Cooked white rice

Place 1-1/2 cups water in slow cooker. Slowly add Crockery Gourmet™ for Beef to water, whisking until smooth. *Product will thicken immediately.* Add liver, tomatoes and bay leaf and stir to coat. Place the remaining ingredients (except rice) into slow cooker. Cook on low setting for 7-8 hours until liver is tender. One-half hour before serving, gently stir all ingredients together. Serve with hot rice.

# Notes

# Notes

# CROCKERY GOURMET

## SEASONING MIX
## FOR PORK

*Easy To Prepare Meals For Your Slow Cooker*
*Dutch Oven or Roaster*

# Pork Chops

Serves 6

*Crockery Gourmet™ for Pork*
*6 pork chops*
*1 red pepper, diced*
*1 green pepper, diced*
*1 onion, sliced*
*4 oz sliced mushrooms*
*Salt and freshly ground black*
*    pepper, to taste*
*Cooked herbed rice and asparagus*

Place 1-1/2 cups water in slow cooker. Slowly add Crockery Gourmet™ for Pork to water, whisking until smooth. *Product will thicken immediately.* Add chops and stir to coat. Place the remaining ingredients (except rice and asparagus) into slow cooker on top of chops. Cook on low setting for 7-8 hours until pork chops are tender and fully cooked. One-half hour before serving, gently stir all ingredients together. Salt and pepper to taste. Serve with herbed rice and steamed asparagus.

*Recipes Using* CROCKERY GOURMET™
SEASONING MIX FOR PORK

The following recipes feature CROCKERY GOURMET™
SEASONING MIX FOR PORK. When cooking pork or lamb, it
is best to trim off the excess fat before placing the meat into
the slow cooker. Slow cooking helps retain the natural meat
juices and especially flavors. Using Crockery Gourmet™ in
your recipes quickly turns these juices into tasty gravies and
sauces.

# Pork Roast with Currants

Serves 4

*Crockery Gourmet™ for Pork*
*2 lbs pork loin roast studded*
*with cloves*
*1 cup applesauce*
*1 cup dried currants*
*1 tsp freshly ground black pepper*
*1 cup sherry*
*2 medium potatoes, peeled and*
*cubed*
*1 medium onion, chopped*
*2 carrots, chopped*
*Cooked polenta or wild rice*

Place 2 cups water in slow cooker. Slowly add Crockery Gourmet™ for Pork to water, whisking until smooth. *Product will thicken immediately.* Add next five ingredients and stir to coat. Place the vegetables into slow cooker. Cook on low setting for 7-8 hours or on high setting for 3-4 hours, until pork is tender. One-half hour before serving, gently stir all ingredients together. Serve with polenta or wild rice.

# Barbecued Turkey Legs

Serves 2

*Crockery Gourmet™ for Pork*
*2 turkey legs, skinned*
*2 cups barbecue sauce*
*1 onion, sliced*

Place 2 cups water in slow cooker. Slowly add Crockery Gourmet™ for Pork to water, whisking until smooth. *Product will thicken immediately.* Place the remaining ingredients into slow cooker, stirring to coat. Cook on low setting for 7-8 hours or on high setting for 3-4 hours, until turkey is tender.

# Pozole

*Crockery Gourmet™ for Pork*
*4 lbs pork loin roast, cut into*
*    chunks*
*2 cloves garlic, minced*
*Juice of two limes*
*1/2 cup chopped italian parsley*
*1 bay leaf*
*1/2 cup red wine*
*2 medium onions, chopped*
*2 1-lb cans yellow hominy*
*1 1-lb can diced tomatoes*

Place 2 cups water in slow cooker. Slowly add Crockery Gourmet™ for Pork to water, whisking until smooth. *Product will thicken immediately.* Add next six ingredients and stir to coat. Place the remaining ingredients into slow cooker. Cook on low setting for 8-9 hours or on high setting for 4-5 hours, until pork roast is tender and comes apart easily. One-half hour before serving, gently stir all ingredients together. Serve as a main course stew with a side salad and bread.

# Pork Roast With Vegetables

Serves 6

*Crockery Gourmet™ for Pork*
*2-3 lbs pork roast, trimmed*
*3-4 medium carrots, halved*
*1 large onion, diced*
*3-4 potatoes, quartered*
*Salt and freshly ground black*
  *pepper, to taste*

Place 2 cups water in slow cooker. Slowly add Crockery Gourmet™ for Pork to water, whisking until smooth. *Product will thicken immediately.* Add roast and coat with sauce. Place the vegetables into slow cooker. Cook on low setting for 7-8 hours until pork roast is tender and fully cooked. One-half hour before serving, gently stir all ingredients together. Salt and pepper to taste.

**Sweet and Sour Pork:** Substitute 1 cup catsup and 1 cup water for 2 cups water. Cut pork into 1-inch cubes, add 1/3 cup sugar and stir to coat. Replace potatoes with 1 medium green pepper, diced. Cook as described above. Serve with rice.

# Ham Hocks and Beans

*Crockery Gourmet™ for Pork*
*2-3 ham hocks*
*2 Tbs chopped cilantro*
*2 Tbs vinegar*
*1 small potato, diced*
*1 onion, diced*
*1 red pepper, diced*
*3 8-oz cans black beans*
*2 Tbs vinegar*
*2 Tbs chopped cilantro*
*1/4 tsp freshly ground black pepper*
*Salt and freshly ground black*
*pepper, to taste*

Place 2 cups water in slow cooker. Slowly add Crockery Gourmet™ for Pork to water, whisking until smooth. *Product will thicken immediately.* Add ham hocks, 2 Tbs chopped cilantro and 2 Tbs vinegar and stir to coat. Place the potato, onion and red pepper into slow cooker. Cook on low setting for 6-7 hours until ham hocks are tender. Gently stir in remaining ingredients. Continue cooking on low setting an additional 30 minutes. Salt and additional pepper to taste.

# Pork Chops with Dates and Nuts

Serves 4

*Crockery Gourmet™ for Pork*
*8 center cut pork chops*
*2 cups pitted dates, chopped*
*1 cup pecans or walnuts,*
*    chopped*
*1 medium onion, chopped*
*2 cloves garlic, chopped*
*1 cup apple juice*
*1 Tbs apple cider vinegar*
*1 tsp freshly ground black pepper*
*1/2 cup chopped italian parsley*
*Cooked rice or potatoes*

Place 2 cups water in slow cooker. Slowly add Crockery Gourmet™ for Pork to water, whisking until smooth. *Product will thicken immediately.* Place the remaining ingredients (except rice or potatoes) into slow cooker, stirring to coat. Cook on low setting for 7-8 hours or on high setting for 3-4 hours, until pork chops are tender. Serve with rice or potatoes.

# *L*amb Shoulder *R*oast

Serves 4

*Crockery Gourmet™ for Pork*
*4 lbs boneless lamb shoulder*
*    roast*
*2 tsp rosemary*
*2 bay leaves*
*1 onion, chopped*
*3 Tbs sugar*
*1 8-oz pkg frozen peas*
*1 cup sherry*
*Mashed potatoes*

Place 2 cups water in slow cooker.  Slowly add Crockery Gourmet™ for Pork to water, whisking until smooth. *Product will thicken immediately.*  Place the remaining ingredients (except mashed potatoes) into slow cooker, stirring to coat.  Cook on low setting for 8-9 hours or on high setting for 4-5 hours, until lamb is tender.  Serve with mashed potatoes.

# Smoked Sausage and *B*eans

Serves 4

*Crockery Gourmet™ for Pork*
*1 lb smoked sausage or kielbasa*
*2 8-oz can white northern beans*
*    with liquid*
*1 bunch green onions, chopped*
*1 carrot, thinly sliced*
*1 Tbs hot pepper vinegar*

Place 2 cups water in slow cooker.  Slowly add Crockery Gourmet™ for Pork to water, whisking until smooth. *Product will thicken immediately.*  Place the remaining ingredients into slow cooker, stirring to coat.  Cook on low setting for 5-6 hours.

# Eggplant Pork Stew

Serves 6

*Crockery Gourmet™ for Pork*
*3 lb pork roast, trimmed*
*1/4 tsp freshly ground black pepper*
*2 cloves garlic, minced*
*1 green pepper, julienned*
*1 red pepper, julienned*
*2 eggplant, peeled and cubed*
*4 potatoes, peeled and quartered*
*2 medium onions, chopped*

Place 2 cups water in slow cooker. Slowly add Crockery Gourmet™ for Pork to water, whisking until smooth. *Product will thicken immediately.* Add pork, pepper and garlic and stir to coat. Place the vegetables into slow cooker. Cook on low setting for 9-10 hours, until pork is tender and cooked through. One-half hour before serving, gently stir all ingredients together.

# Lemon Herbed Pork Roast

Serves 6-8

*Crockery Gourmet™ for Pork*
*3-4 lb pork or ham roast,*
    *trimmed*
*1/8 tsp freshly ground black pepper*
*2 cloves garlic, minced*
*1-1/2 tsp thyme*
*1-1/2 tsp ground sage*
*2 tsp lemon zest*
*1 small onion, minced*

Place 2 cups water in slow cooker. Slowly add Crockery Gourmet™ for Pork to water, whisking until smooth. *Product will thicken immediately.* Place the remaining ingredients into slow cooker, stirring to coat. Cook on low setting for 9-10 hours, until pork is tender and cooked through.

# *C*arnitas

*Crockery Gourmet™ for Pork*
*2 lbs pork loin roast*
*2 onions, chopped*
*1 carrot, chopped*
*1 bell pepper, chopped*
*2 cloves garlic, minced*
*1 Tbs Better Than Bouillon™*
    *Chili Base*
*1 tsp oregano*
*1 bunch cilantro, chopped*
*1 4-oz can green chilies, chopped*

Place 3 cups water in slow cooker. Slowly add Crockery Gourmet™ for Pork to water, whisking until smooth. *Product will thicken immediately.* Place the remaining ingredients into slow cooker, stirring to coat. Cook on low setting for 8-9 hours or on high setting for 4-5 hours, until pork is very tender. Serve with rice and warm tortillas.

# *M*ixed *S*weet and *S*our *B*eans

Serves 6-8

*Crockery Gourmet™ for Pork*
*5 slices bacon, diced*
*1/2 cup diced green pepper*
*1 onion, chopped*
*1/3 cup brown sugar*
*1 tsp prepared mustard*
*2 cloves garlic, minced*
*1/4 cup vinegar*
*1 1-lb can lima beans, drained*
*1 1-lb can baked beans, drained*
*1 1-lb can kidney beans, drained*
*1 tsp Better Than Bouillon™ Ham*
    *Base (optional)*

Place 2 cups water in slow cooker. Slowly add Crockery Gourmet™ for Pork to water, whisking until smooth. *Product will thicken immediately.* Place the remaining ingredients into slow cooker, stirring to coat. Cook on low setting for 6-7 hours.

# *H*ot *H*ot *H*ot *S*pareribs

Serves 4

*Crockery Gourmet™ for Pork*
*4 lbs spareribs*
*4 fresh jalapenos, seeded and*
    *chopped*
*1 Tbs cayenne pepper*
*1 cup catsup*
*1 tsp brown sugar*

Place 2 cups water in slow cooker. Slowly add Crockery Gourmet™ for Pork to water, whisking until smooth. *Product will thicken immediately.* Stir in the remaining ingredients, except ribs. Submerge ribs in sauce. Cook on low setting for 8-10 until ribs are tender.

# *7*ruit and Spice *L*amb Shanks

*Crockery Gourmet™ for Pork*
*4 lamb shanks*
*1/4 tsp freshly ground black pepper*
*1 cup dried apricots*
*1 cup pitted prunes*
*2 tsp vinegar*
*1/3 cup water*
*1/3 cup sugar*
*1/2 tsp ground allspice*
*1/2 tsp ground cinnamon*
*1/4 tsp ground cloves*
*Cooked rice*

Place 2 cups water in slow cooker. Slowly add Crockery Gourmet™ for Pork to water, whisking until smooth. *Product will thicken immediately.* Sprinkle the lamb shanks with pepper and place into slow cooker. Add fruit, stirring to coat. In a separate bowl, combine remaining ingredients (except rice) and pour over lamb and fruit. Cook on low setting for 8-9 hours until lamb is tender. Serve with rice.

# 7urkey with Raisins & 7arragon

Serves 4

*Crockery Gourmet™ for Pork*
*3-4 lb turkey breast*
*1 onion, sliced*
*1 carrot, sliced*
*1/4 cup fresh tarragon leaves*
*1 lb golden raisins*
*1/2 cup chopped italian parsley*
*Freshly ground black pepper, to*
  *taste*

Place 2 cups water in slow cooker. Slowly add Crockery Gourmet™ for Pork to water, whisking until smooth. *Product will thicken immediately.* Place the remaining ingredients into slow cooker, stirring to coat. Cook on low setting for 7-8 hours or on high setting for 3-4 hours, until turkey is tender.

# Crown Roast of Pork

Serves 4

*Crockery Gourmet™ for Pork*
*3-lb crown pork roast, tied and*
  *standing*
*2 cups sherry*
*1 lb pearl onions, peeled*
*Cooked rice or baked potatoes*

Place 2 cups water in slow cooker. Slowly add Crockery Gourmet™ for Pork to water, whisking until smooth. *Product will thicken immediately.* Stir in sherry. Stand the roast in the slow cooker and fill center with onions. Cook on low setting for 7-8 hours. Serve with rice or potatoes.

# $\mathcal{A}$corn $\mathcal{C}$hops

*Crockery Gourmet™ for Pork*
*6 pork chops, trimmed*
*2 medium acorn squash, cut into*
*    8-10 wedges*
*2 Tbs unsalted butter, melted*
*3/4 cup brown sugar*
*1/2 tsp Better Than Bouillon™*
*    Beef Base or concentrated beef*
*    stock*
*1 Tbs orange juice*
*1/2 tsp orange zest*
*1/2 cup water*

Place 1-1/2 cups water in slow cooker. Slowly add Crockery Gourmet™ for Pork to water, whisking until smooth. *Product will thicken immediately.* Place 3 chops in one layer into slow cooker. Layer squash over chops. Place the remaining chops onto squash. In a separate bowl, combine remaining ingredients and pour over chops. Cook on low setting for 5-6 hours, until pork is tender and cooked through.

# £amb Stew

Serves 6

*Crockery Gourmet™ for Pork*
*1-1/2 lbs lamb, cut into 2-inch*
*cubes*
*Freshly ground black pepper*
*1/4 tsp crushed marjoram*
*1/8 tsp thyme*
*2 medium onions, chopped*
*2 ribs celery, chopped*
*3 medium potatoes, peeled and*
*thinly sliced*
*1 8-oz pkg frozen peas*
*4 Tbs flour dissolved in 1/2 cup*
*water*

Place 2 cups water in slow cooker. Slowly add Crockery Gourmet™ for Pork to water, whisking until smooth. *Product will thicken immediately.* Sprinkle the lamb with pepper, marjoram and thyme, place into slow cooker and stir to coat. Place the vegetables into slow cooker. Cook on low setting for 7-8 hours until lamb and potatoes are tender. Add peas and flour mixture to thicken sauce, gently stirring all ingredients together. Cook on high 10-15 minutes and serve.

# Venison Pot Roast

Serves 4

*Crockery Gourmet™ for Pork*
*3-lb venison shoulder roast*
*1 cup dry sherry*
*1 large onion, chopped*
*3 carrots, chopped*
*4 large potatoes, chopped*

Place 2 cups water in slow cooker. Slowly add Crockery Gourmet™ for Pork to water, whisking until smooth. *Product will thicken immediately.* Add venison and sherry and stir to coat. Place the vegetables into slow cooker. Cook on low setting for 7-8 hours. One-half hour before serving, gently stir all ingredients together.

# Blackeyed Peas and Sausage

Serves 4

*Crockery Gourmet™ for Pork*
*1 lb dried blackeyed peas, soaked*
*    overnight*
*1-1/2 lb smoked sausage, cut into*
*    1/2-inch pieces*
*2 bay leaves*
*1 large onion, chopped*
*1 tsp freshly ground black pepper*
*1/4 cup hot pepper vinegar*
*Cooked rice or potatoes*

Place 2 cups water in slow cooker. Slowly add Crockery Gourmet™ for Pork to water, whisking until smooth. *Product will thicken immediately.* Stir in an additional 2 cups water and place the remaining ingredients (except rice or potatoes) into slow cooker, stirring to coat. Cook on low setting for 7-8 hours, checking after 4 hours to see if additional water is needed. Add water as necessary. Serve with rice or potatoes.

# Hot Knockwurst and Potatoes

Serves 6

*Crockery Gourmet™ for Pork*
*6 knockwurst, sliced 1/4-inch*
*thick*
*2 slices bacon, diced*
*1 ribs celery, diced*
*1 onion, sliced*
*4 large potatoes, peeled and*
*quartered*
*2 Tbs sugar*
*1 tsp dry mustard*
*1/4 tsp freshly ground black pepper*
*1/3 cup vinegar*
*1/4 cup water*

Place 2 cups water in slow cooker. Slowly add Crockery Gourmet™ for Pork to water, whisking until smooth. *Product will thicken immediately.* Add knockwurst and stir to coat. Place the bacon, celery, onion and potatoes into slow cooker. Combine the remaining ingredients in a separate bowl and pour over meat and vegetables. Cook on low setting for 5-6 hour until potatoes are tender. One-half hour before serving, gently stir all ingredients together. Serve warm and garnish with chopped italian parsley.

# *L*amb *R*ibs

*Crockery Gourmet™ for Pork*
*2 lbs lamb ribs, separated*
*1 large eggplant, peeled and*
    *cubed*
*1 red pepper, chopped*
*1 green pepper, chopped*
*1 onion, chopped*
*Salt and freshly ground black*
    *pepper, to taste*
*Cooked rice*

Place 1-1/2 cups water in slow cooker. Slowly add
Crockery Gourmet™ for Pork to water, whisking until
smooth. *Product will thicken immediately.* Add ribs and
stir to coat. Place the remaining ingredients into slow
cooker. Cook on low setting for 6-8 hours until rib meat
is tender. One-half hour before serving, gently stir all
ingredients together. Salt and pepper to taste. Serve
over rice.

# ℋam and 𝒫otato 𝒮oup

Serves 4

    *Crockery Gourmet™ for Pork*
    *1 lb smoked ham, cubed*
    *1 lb yukon gold potatoes, cubed*
    *1 large onion, chopped*
    *1 Tbs dill weed*
    *1/4 tsp peppers*
    *1 cup white wine*
    *1  10-oz can evaporated milk*
    *Crackers or bread*

Place 2 cups water in slow cooker. Slowly add Crockery Gourmet™ for Pork to water, whisking until smooth. *Product will thicken immediately.* Place the remaining ingredients (except crackers or bread) into slow cooker, stirring to coat. Cook on low setting for 7-8 hours or on high setting for 3-4 hours, until potatoes are soft. Serve with crackers or bread.

# 𝒫orky 𝒢oes

Serves 6

    *Crockery Gourmet™ for Pork*
    *2 lb pork rump roast*
    *1 large onion, thinly sliced*
    *1 cup barbecue sauce*
    *1 Tbs worcestershire*
    *2 Tbs brown sugar*
    *1 tsp liquid smoke*
    *Sesame buns*

Place 2 cups water in slow cooker. Slowly add Crockery Gourmet™ for Pork to water, whisking until smooth. *Product will thicken immediately.* Place the remaining ingredients (except buns) into slow cooker, stirring to coat. Cook on low setting for 8-9 hours or on high setting for 4-5 hours, until pork roast shreds easily from the bone. Serve on toasted sesame buns.

# 𝒯urkey 𝐵reast with 𝒜pples

*Crockery Gourmet™ for Pork*
*3-4 lbs turkey breast, skinless*
*2 cups apple juice*
*4 tart apples, cored and sliced*
*1 red bell pepper, julienned*
*1 green bell pepper, julienned*
*1 yellow bell pepper, julienned*
*1 medium onion, sliced*
*Cooked brown or white rice*

Place 2 cups water in slow cooker. Slowly add Crockery Gourmet™ for Pork to water, whisking until smooth. *Product will thicken immediately.* Add turkey and apple juice and stir to coat. Place the remaining ingredients (except rice) into slow cooker. Cook on low setting for 7-8 hours or on high setting for 3-4 hours. One-half hour before serving, gently stir all ingredients together. Serve with brown or white rice.

# Marmalade Pork Roast

Serves 6

*1/4 cup orange marmalade*
*1/8 cup molasses*
*1/8 cup yellow mustard*
*1/4 cup vinegar*
*1/4 tsp ground ginger*

*Crockery Gourmet™ for Pork*
*3 lb pork roast*
*1/8 tsp freshly ground black pepper*
*4 carrots, chopped*
*1 large onion, chopped*
*4 medium potatoes, quartered*

In a small bowl, combine marmalade, molasses, mustard, vinegar and ginger. Set aside. Place 2 cups water in slow cooker. Slowly add Crockery Gourmet™ for Pork to water, whisking until smooth. *Product will thicken immediately.* Sprinkle roast with pepper and place in slow cooker, stirring to coat. Spread marmalade mixture over roast. Place the vegetables on top of the roast Cook on low setting for 8-9 hours until pork roast is tender and cooked through.

# Notes

# Vegetarian, Low-fat & Non-fat

*Recipes Using* CROCKERY GOURMET™ SEASONING MIXES

The following recipes feature all three CROCKERY GOURMET™ SEASONING MIXES. Crockery Gourmet™ seasonings are perfect for low-fat and vegetarian cooking. They bring out the flavor of all vegetables, but do not add any actual meat or meat juices to the dish. For reference, the low-fat and non-fat recipes provide the number of calories and grams of fat per serving.

# Dijon Chicken

Serves 6

Crockery Gourmet™ for Chicken
4 boneless, skinless chicken
   breasts, cubed
1 Tbs dijon mustard
1 bunch green onions, chopped
1 tsp dijon mustard ·
1/4 tsp freshly ground pepper
Cooked rice

Place 1-1/2 cups water in slow cooker. Slowly add
Crockery Gourmet™ for Chicken to water, whisking until
smooth. *Product will thicken immediately.* Place the
chicken, 1 Tbs dijon mustard and green onions into slow
cooker, stirring to coat. Cook on low setting for 7-8
hours until chicken is tender. Just before serving, stir in
1 tsp dijon mustard and pepper. Serve with rice.

*240 calories and 3 grams fat per serving*

# Beefy Mushrooms and Potatoes

Serves 6

Crockery Gourmet™ for Beef
2 lbs mushrooms, sliced
3 large potatoes, slices, unpeeled
2 onions, chopped
1 cup white wine
1 tsp freshly ground black pepper
Salt and freshly ground black
   pepper, to taste

Place 1-1/2 cups water in slow cooker. Slowly add
Crockery Gourmet™ for Beef to water, whisking until
smooth. *Product will thicken immediately.* Place the
remaining ingredients into slow cooker, stirring to coat.
Cook on low setting for 6-7 hours until potatoes are
tender. Salt and additional pepper to taste.

*210 calories and 4 grams fat per serving*

# Pork Roast

*Crockery Gourmet™ for Pork*
*2 lbs pork loin roast*
*1/2 cup raisins*
*2 cloves garlic, minced*
*2 bay leaves*
*6 oz tomato paste*
*1 cup red wine*
*2 onions, chopped*
*2 carrots, coarsely chopped*
*2 ribs celery, coarsely chopped*
*2 potatoes, cut into large cubes*
*Salt and freshly ground black*
*pepper, to taste*

Place 1-1/2 cups water in slow cooker. Slowly add
Crockery Gourmet™ for Pork to water, whisking until
smooth. *Product will thicken immediately.* Add roast and
next five ingredients and stir to coat. Place the vegetables into slow cooker. Cook on low setting for 9-10
hours until pork roast is tender. One-half hour before
serving, gently stir all ingredients together. Salt and
pepper to taste.

*220 calories and 8 grams fat per serving*

# French Onion Soup

Serves 6

*Crockery Gourmet™ for Beef*
*3 onions, sliced*
*2 cups red wine*
*5 cups Better Than Bouillon™*
    *beef stock*
*1/2 tsp freshly ground pepper*
*6 Tbs non-fat mozzarella*

Place 1-1/2 cups water in slow cooker. Slowly add Crockery Gourmet™ for Beef to water, whisking until smooth. *Product will thicken immediately.* Place the onions, wine, beef stock and pepper into slow cooker, stirring to coat. Cook on low setting for 6-7 hours until onions are tender. Salt and additional pepper to taste. Serve hot, sprinkled with 1 Tbs mozzarella.

*130 calories and 0 grams fat per serving*

# Potatoes and Ham

Serves 4

*Crockery Gourmet™ for Pork*
*2 lbs smoked ham, cubed*
*4 medium potatoes, sliced*
*1 large onion, chopped*
*1 Tbs dill weed*
*1/4 tsp white pepper*
*2 tsp Better Than Bouillon™*
    *Chicken Base dissolved in*
    *2 cups hot water*
*1/2 cup sherry*

Place 1-1/2 cups water in slow cooker. Slowly add Crockery Gourmet™ for Pork to water, whisking until smooth. *Product will thicken immediately.* Place the remaining ingredients into slow cooker, stirring to coat. Cook on low setting for 7-8 hours until potatoes are tender.

*180 calories and 8 grams fat per serving*

# Green Chili Beef

*Crockery Gourmet™ for Beef*
*2-3 lbs lean beef chuck roast,*
*    trimmed and cubed*
*3 Tbs flour*
*1 small can green chilies,*
*    chopped*
*1 small can pimentos*
*1 clove garlic, minced*
*2 Tbs chili powder*
*1 tsp oregano*
*1/2 tsp cumin*
*1/2 tsp freshly ground pepper*
*2 Tbs catsup*
*1 cup red wine*
*1 onion, chopped*
*1 green pepper, chopped*

Place 1-1/2 cups water in slow cooker. Slowly add Crockery Gourmet™ for Beef to water, whisking until smooth. *Product will thicken immediately.* In a separate bowl, coat the beef with the flour. Place beef and next nine ingredients in slow cooker and stir to coat. Place the vegetables on top of the beef. Cook on low setting for 8-9 hours until beef is tender. One-half hour before serving, gently stir all ingredients together.

***210 calories and 8 grams fat per serving***

# Pork and Apples

Serves 6

Crockery Gourmet™ for Pork
2-3 lbs pork loin roast
2 onions, chopped
3 carrots, thinly sliced
3 rome or cooking apples, cored,
    peeled and sliced
1 tsp sugar
Salt and freshly ground black
    pepper, to taste
Cooked rice

Place 1-1/2 cups water in slow cooker. Slowly add
Crockery Gourmet™ for Pork to water, whisking until
smooth. *Product will thicken immediately.* Add roast and
stir to coat. Place remaining ingredients (except salt,
pepper and rice) into slow cooker. Cook on low setting
for 8-10 hours until pork roast is tender. One-half hour
before serving, gently stir all ingredients together. Salt
and pepper to taste. Serve with rice.

*200 calories and 8 grams fat per serving*

# *C*reamy *P*otatoes

*Crockery Gourmet™ for Chicken*
*2 lbs potatoes, sliced*
*1 cup chopped green onions*
*1/2 cup chopped italian parsley*
*1 clove garlic, chopped*
*2 tsp mixed dried herbs*
*4 tsp Better Than Bouillon™*
  *Chicken Base or concentrated*
  *stock dissolved in 4 cups hot*
  *water*
*2 Tbs flour*
*1 cup non-fat evaporated milk,*
  *warm*
*4 tsp non-fat parmesan cheese*
  *(optional)*
*Salt and white pepper, to taste*

Place 1-1/2 cups water in slow cooker. Slowly add Crockery Gourmet™ for Chicken to water, whisking until smooth. *Product will thicken immediately.* Place the next six ingredients into slow cooker and stir to coat. Cook on low setting for 3-4 hours until potatoes are tender. One-half hour before serving, dissolve flour in warm milk and add to potatoes. Stir in cheese, if desired. Salt and pepper to taste.

*175 calories and 3.5 grams fat per serving*

# Meatless Beef Stew

Serves 6

*Crockery Gourmet™ for Beef*
*2 onions, coarsely chopped*
*2 carrots, coarsely chopped*
*3 potatoes, coarsely chopped*
*2 ribs celery, chopped*
*2 zucchini, chopped*
*1/2 cup chopped italian parsley*
*1 lb mushrooms*
*1 bay leaf*
*1 clove garlic, minced*
*1 tsp Better Than Bouillon™ Beef*
*    Base or seasoned salt*
*1 cup red wine*
*1/2 cup water*

Place 1-1/2 cups water in slow cooker. Slowly add Crockery Gourmet™ for Beef to water, whisking until smooth. *Product will thicken immediately.* Place the next eight ingredients into slow cooker. In a separate bowl, dissolve Better Than Bouillon™ Beef Base into red wine and water and add to slow cooker. Stir to coat all ingredients and cook on low setting for 3-4 hours until vegetables are tender. Salt and pepper to taste.

*150 calories and 0 grams fat per serving*

# Chicken Corn Soup

*Crockery Gourmet™ for Chicken*
*2 boneless, skinless chicken*
*    breasts, cubed*
*1 onion, chopped*
*2 carrots, sliced*
*2 ribs celery, chopped*
*2 medium potatoes, cut into large*
*    cubes*
*1 tsp mixed dried herbs*
*1/3 cup tomato sauce*
*1 large can cream style corn*
*1 small can whole kernel corn*
*2 cups Better Than Bouillon™*
*    chicken stock*
*1/4 cup chopped italian parsley*
*Salt and freshly ground black*
*    pepper, to taste*

Place 1-1/2 cups water in slow cooker. Slowly add Crockery Gourmet™ for Chicken to water, whisking until smooth. *Product will thicken immediately.* Place the remaining ingredients (except parsley, salt and pepper) into slow cooker, stirring to coat. Cook on low setting for 8-9 hours until chicken is tender. Add parsley 1/2 hour before serving. Salt and pepper to taste.

*320 calories and 2.5 grams fat per serving*

# Barley and Beef

Serves 6

*Crockery Gourmet™ for Beef*
*1/2 lb pearl barley*
*1 onion, chopped*
*2 carrots, chopped*
*1 bay leaf*
*1 clove garlic, minced*
*1 cup red wine*
*3-1/2 cups water*
*2 tsp mixed dried herbs*
*Salt and freshly ground black*
*     pepper, to taste*

Place 1-1/2 cups water in slow cooker. Slowly add Crockery Gourmet™ for Beef to water, whisking until smooth. *Product will thicken immediately.* Place the remaining ingredients (except salt and pepper) into slow cooker, stirring to coat. Cook on low setting for 7-8 hours until barley is tender. Salt and pepper to taste.

*230 calories and 3 grams fat per serving*

# Orange Parsnip Stew

Serves 4-6

*Crockery Gourmet™ for Chicken*
*8-10 medium parsnips, peeled*
*     and cut into 1/4-inch sticks*
*2 Tbs unsalted butter, melted*
*2 Tbs honey*
*Juice of 1 large orange*
*1 tsp orange zest*

Place 2 cups water in slow cooker. Slowly add Crockery Gourmet™ for Chicken to water, whisking until smooth. *Product will thicken immediately.* Place the parsnips into slow cooker, stirring to coat. In a separate bowl, combine remaining ingredients and pour over parsnips. Cook on low setting for 3-4 hours until parsnips are tender.

# Turkey Stew

Serves 4

*Crockery Gourmet™ for Chicken*
*2 lbs turkey breast, cubed*
*1 clove garlic, minced*
*1/4 cup sherry*
*1 large potato, cubed*
*1 onion, chopped*
*2 carrots, chopped*
*2 ribs celery, chopped*
*Salt and freshly ground black*
*pepper, to taste*

Place 1-1/2 cups water in slow cooker. Slowly add Crockery Gourmet™ for Chicken to water, whisking until smooth. *Product will thicken immediately.* Add turkey, garlic and sherry and stir to coat. Place the vegetables into slow cooker. Cook on low setting for 7-8 hours until turkey is tender. One-half hour before serving, gently stir all ingredients together. Salt and pepper to taste.

*240 calories and 2.5 grams fat per serving*

# Salsa Verde

Serves 6

*Crockery Gourmet™ for Chicken*
*2 lbs tomatillos, hulled and*
*chopped*
*1 large onion, chopped*
*3 cloves garlic, minced*
*1 bunch cilantro, chopped*
*Chips*

Place 2 cups water in slow cooker. Slowly add Crockery Gourmet™ for Chicken to water, whisking until smooth. *Product will thicken immediately.* Place the remaining ingredients (except chips) into slow cooker, stirring to coat. Cook on low setting for 4-6 hours. Serve warm or cold with chips.

# Savory Eye of Round

Serves 4

*Crockery Gourmet™ for Beef*
*2 lbs eye of round, trimmed*
*1 onion, chopped*
*2 cloves garlic, chopped*
*2 ribs celery, chopped*
*3 Tbs dark corn syrup*
*1/2 tsp red pepper*
*1/2 tsp ginger*
*1 cup red wine*
*1 tsp freshly ground black pepper*
*Salt and freshly ground black*
    *pepper, to taste*
*Cooked potatoes or rice*

Place 1-1/2 cups water in slow cooker. Slowly add Crockery Gourmet™ for Beef to water, whisking until smooth. *Product will thicken immediately.* Place the remaining ingredients into slow cooker, stirring to coat. Cook on low setting for 9-10 hours until beef roast is tender. Salt and pepper to taste. Serve with potatoes or rice.

*240 calories and 8 grams fat per serving*

# Ham and Butter Beans

Serves 4

*Crockery Gourmet™ for Pork*
*2 lbs smoked ham, cubed*
*3 cans butter beans, drained*
*2 bunches green onions, chopped*
*1 tsp freshly ground black pepper*
*Salt and freshly ground black*
    *pepper, to taste*
*Cooked rice or pasta*

Place 1-1/2 cups water in slow cooker. Slowly add Crockery Gourmet™ for Pork to water, whisking until smooth. *Product will thicken immediately.* Place the remaining ingredients into slow cooker, stirring to coat. Cook on low setting for 3-4 hours. Salt and additional pepper to taste. Serve with rice or pasta.

**240 calories and 8 grams fat per serving**

# Baby Carrots in Dilled Sauce

Serves 4

*Crockery Gourmet™ for Chicken*
*2 lbs baby carrots, halved*
*1/2 cup white wine*
*1-1/2 tsp fresh dill, minced*
*1/2 cup minced onion*
*1 clove garlic, crushed*
*1 Tbs lemon juice*
*2 Tbs cornstarch dissolved in 2*
    *Tbs cold water*

Place 1-1/2 cups water and wine in slow cooker. Slowly add Crockery Gourmet™ for Chicken to water, whisking until smooth. *Product will thicken immediately.* Place all ingredients (except cornstarch mixture) into slow cooker, stirring to coat. Cook on low setting for 3-4 hours until carrots are tender. Whisk in the cornstarch mixture to thicken sauce 10 minutes before serving.

# Summer Squash

Serves 4

*Crockery Gourmet™ for Chicken*
*1 lb summer squash, ends*
   *trimmed*
*2 small tomatoes, peeled and*
   *chopped*
*1/2 green pepper, chopped*
*1/2 cup sliced green onions*
*1 tsp mixed fresh herbs, minced*
*1/8 tsp freshly ground black pepper*

Place 2 cups water in slow cooker. Slowly add Crockery Gourmet™ for Chicken to water, whisking until smooth. *Product will thicken immediately.* Place the remaining ingredients into slow cooker, stirring to coat. Cook on low setting for 4-5 hours until squash is tender.

*Note:* Add 1 Tbs vegetarian bacon bits for added flavor.

# Garlic Tomato Soup

Serves 6

*Crockery Gourmet™ for Beef*
*6 cloves garlic, minced*
*1 Tbs paprika*
*3 cups canned puréed tomatoes*
*Hearty bread*

Place 2 cups water in slow cooker. Slowly add Crockery Gourmet™ for Beef to water, whisking until smooth. *Product will thicken immediately.* Place additional 3 cups water and the remaining ingredients (except bread) into slow cooker, stirring to coat. Cook on low setting for 3-4 hours. Serve with hearty bread.

# Zucchini Stew

Serves 4-6

Crockery Gourmet™ for Pork
2 lbs zucchini, cut into 1/2-inch
    medallions
1 green pepper, chopped
1 medium onion, chopped
2 cloves garlic, minced
1/4 tsp freshly ground black pepper
4 tomatoes, peeled and chopped
    or 1 16-oz can chopped
    tomatoes
2 Tbs minced italian parsley
1 tsp basil

Place 1-1/2 cups water in slow cooker. Slowly add Crockery Gourmet™ for Pork to water, whisking until smooth. *Product will thicken immediately.* Place the remaining ingredients into slow cooker, stirring to coat. Cook on low setting for 2-3 hours until zucchini is tender.

# Great Green Beans

Serves 4

Crockery Gourmet™ for Chicken
1 lb fresh green beans
2 Tbs olive oil
1/2 cup chopped italian parsley
2 cups diced fresh tomatoes
2 tsp white pepper

Place 2 cups water in slow cooker. Slowly add Crockery Gourmet™ for Pork to water, whisking until smooth. *Product will thicken immediately.* Place the remaining ingredients into slow cooker, stirring to coat. Cook on low setting for 3-4 hours.

# *C*reole *E*ggplant

Serves 4

*Crockery Gourmet™ for Chicken*
*2 large eggplants, peeled and*
*    chopped*
*1 large onion, chopped*
*1 green pepper, chopped*
*1 red bell pepper, chopped*
*2 ribs celery, chopped*
*4 cloves garlic, minced*
*1-lb can chopped tomatoes with*
*    liquid*

Place 2 cups water in slow cooker. Slowly add Crockery
Gourmet™ for Pork to water, whisking until smooth.
*Product will thicken immediately.* Place the remaining
ingredients into slow cooker, stirring to coat. Cook on
low setting for 5-6 hours. Serve with rice.

# *T*omato *C*hutney

Serves 2

*Crockery Gourmet™ for Beef*
*2 lb ripe tomatoes, chopped*
*1 medium onion, chopped*
*1/2 cup golden raisins*
*1/3 cup grown sugar*
*1/4 cup honey*
*1 tsp ginger*
*1 cup cider vinegar*
*1 tsp chili powder*
*Toast*

Place 2 cups water in slow cooker. Slowly add Crockery
Gourmet™ for Beef to water, whisking until smooth.
*Product will thicken immediately.* Place the remaining
ingredients into slow cooker, stirring to coat. Cook on
low setting for 3-5 hours. Serve warm or cold with toast.

# 7omato Stew

Serves 6

*Crockery Gourmet™ for Chicken*
*2 lbs zucchini, sliced into rounds*
*4 cloves garlic, minced*
*1 medium onion, chopped*
*1 carrot, chopped*
*1 green pepper, chopped*
*1 tsp coriander*
*1 tsp freshly ground black pepper*
*4 large tomatoes, chopped*
*1 lb mushrooms, sliced*

Place 2 cups water in slow cooker. Slowly add Crockery Gourmet™ for Chicken to water, whisking until smooth. *Product will thicken immediately.* Place the remaining ingredients into slow cooker, stirring to coat. Cook on low setting for 5-6 hours. Serve as a first course soup.

# Stewed Eggplant

Serves 4

*Crockery Gourmet™ for Beef*
*1 large onion, minced*
*2 large eggplants, peeled and*
*    cubed*
*2 cloves garlic, minced*
*1 cup tomato purée*
*1 tsp oregano*
*1 tsp freshly ground black pepper*

Place 2 cups water in slow cooker. Slowly add Crockery Gourmet™ for Beef to water, whisking until smooth. *Product will thicken immediately.* Place the remaining ingredients into slow cooker, stirring to coat. Cook on low setting for 4-5 hours. Serve over rice or as a side dish.

# *C*urried *C*hicken

Serves 6

*Crockery Gourmet™ for Chicken*
*4 boneless, skinless chicken*
*breasts, cubed*
*2 Tbs curry powder*
*1 cup pineapple juice*
*1 lb mushrooms, sliced*
*1/2 tsp hot sauce*
*1/2 cup pineapple juice*

Place 1-1/2 cups water in slow cooker. Slowly add
Crockery Gourmet™ for Chicken to water, whisking until
smooth. *Product will thicken immediately.* Place all but
1/2 cup pineapple juice into slow cooker, stirring to coat.
Cook on low setting for 7-8 hours until chicken is tender.
Add 1/2 cup pineapple juice 10 minutes before serving.
Salt and pepper to taste. Serve with rice.

*250 calories and 3 grams fat per serving*

# *S*weet *P*otatoes and *A*pples

Serves 6

*Crockery Gourmet™ for Pork*
*6 medium sweet potatoes, peeled*
*and cut into bite-sized pieces*
*4 granny smith apples, peeled,*
*cored and sliced 1/2-inch thick*
*1 tsp sugar*
*1/4 cup orange juice*
*1 Tbs grated orange zest*

Place 1-1/2 cups water in slow cooker. Slowly add
Crockery Gourmet™ for Pork to water, whisking until
smooth. *Product will thicken immediately.* Place the
remaining ingredients into slow cooker, stirring to coat.
Cook on low setting for 5-6 hours until potatoes are tender.

# Red Cabbage Delight

*Crockery Gourmet™ for Pork*
*1 tsp Better Than Bouillon™ Ham*
    *Base or concentrated ham*
    *stock*
*1/4 cup brown sugar*
*1/8 tsp freshly ground black pepper*
*1/4 cup white vinegar*
*1 large onion, chopped*
*1 large red cabbage, shredded*
*4 tsp bacon bits*

Place 1-1/2 cups water in slow cooker. Slowly add Crockery Gourmet™ for Pork to water, whisking until smooth. *Product will thicken immediately.* Stir in ham base, sugar, pepper and vinegar. Add onion and caggabe and stir to coat. Cook on low setting for 4-5 hours. Sprinkle with bacon bits and serve.

# Braised Leeks

Serves 6

*Crockery Gourmet™ for Chicken*
*6 large or 12 small leeks, cleaned*
    *and trimmed (see Note)*
*3 Tbs butter*

Place 2 cups water in slow cooker. Slowly add Crockery Gourmet™ for Chicken to water, whisking until smooth. *Product will thicken immediately.* Add leeks and butter and turn to coat. Spread leeks evenly. Cook on low setting for 3-4 hours.

**Note:** To prepare leeks, trim root ends, remove any wilted leaves and cut off tops so leeks are 6-7 inches long. Slit each lengthwise to where the white begins; turn leek 1/4 turn and slit again. Wash thoroughly under running cold water to remove all grit between leaves.

# Stuffed Whole Cabbage

Serves 6-8

2 cups bulgar (cracked wheat)
2 qts hot water
1 cup finely diced carrots
1 cup finely diced onions
1 cup finely diced celery
4 Tbs butter
1 cup chopped raisins
1 egg
1/2 cup ricotta or cream cheese
Juice of 1/2 lemon
Salt and freshly ground black
    pepper, to taste

Crockery Gourmet™ for Chicken
Leaves of one 3-lb cabbage,
    blanched
2 cups tomato sauce, warmed

To prepare stuffing, soak bulgar in hot water 5 minutes. Drain and squeeze dry. Sauté carrots, onions and celery in butter until just cooked. Combine bulgar, cooked vegetables, raisins, egg, cheese and lemon juice and season to taste. (May be prepared in advance.)

Place 2 cups water in slow cooker. Slowly add Crockery Gourmet™ for Chicken to water, whisking until smooth. *Product will thicken immediately.* Line the bottom and sides of the slow cooker with the largest leaves, stems up. Spread with a layer of stuffing and cover with a layer of leaves. Continue alternating stuffing and leaves, ending with a final layer of leaves. Carefully spoon the sauce over the cabbage, adding water until liquid comes halfway up the cabbage. Cook on low setting for 5-6 hours.

Carefully remove and invert entire cabbage onto a serving plate. Stir tomato sauce into cooking liquid and serve with wedges of stuffed cabbage.

# *N*otes

# HERB AND SPICE GUIDE

*Allspice* - a pea-sized fruit that grows in Mexico, Jamaica, Central and South America. It has a delicate flavor which resembles a blend of cloves, cinnamon and nutmeg. Common Uses: whole-pickles, meats, boiled fish, gravies; ground-puddings, relishes, fruit preserves, baking.

*Annato* - an aromatic spice often used instead of saffron. Commonly used in rice and seafood dishes.

*Basil* - the dried leaves and stems of an herb grown in the US and North Mediterranean area. It has an aromatic, leafy flavor. Common Uses: flavoring tomato dishes and sauces, turtle soup, cooked peas, squash, snap beans; sprinkled over lamb and poultry.

*Bay Leaves* - the dried leaves of an evergreen grown in the eastern Mediterranean countries. It has a sweet, herbaceous floral spice note. Common Uses: for pickling, stews, for spicing sauces and soup; also for spicing a variety of meats and fish.

*Caraway* - the seed of a plant grown in the Netherlands. Its flavor combines the tastes of anise and dill. Common Uses: baking breads, often added to sauerkraut, noodles, cheese spreads; adds zest to french fried potatoes, liver, canned asparagus.

*Cinnamon* - the bark of a tree found in Ceylon. Spicy and pungent aroma. Commonly used in baked items, mulled wine and fruit compotes.

*Curry Powder* - a ground blend of ginger, turmeric, fengreek seed, as many as 16 to 20 spices. Common Uses: Indian curry recipes such as lamb, chicken and rice, eggs, vegetables.

*Dill Weed* - the small, dark seed of the dill plant grown in India, having a clean, aromatic taste. Common Uses: a predominant seasoning in pickling recipes; also adds pleasing flavor to sauerkraut, potato salad, cooked macaroni, and fish.

*Filé* - classic thickener for creole gumbos. Tapioca flour may be substituted.

*Marjoram* - an herb of the mint family, grown in France and Chile. It has a minty-sweet flavor. Common Uses: in beverages, jellies and to flavor soups, stews, fish, sauces; also excellent for sprinkling on lamb while roasting.

*Oregano* - the leaf of a safe bush grown in Italy, Greece and Mexico. Common Uses: excellent flavoring for any tomato dish, especially Italian specialities.

*Paprika* - a mild, sweet red pepper grown in Spain, Central Europe and the US. Slightly aromatic and prized for brilliant red color. Common Uses: a colorful garnish for pale foods, and for seasoning goulash and salad dressings.

*Rosemary* - an herb grown in France, Spain and Portugal. It has a sweet, fresh taste. Common Uses: in lamb and chicken dishes, soups, stews.

*Sage* - the leaf of a shrub grown in Greece, Yugoslavia and Albania. Its flavor is camphoraceous and minty. Common Uses: for meat and poultry stuffing, sausages, meat loaf, hamburgers, stews, and salads.

*Savory* - a delicate spice often used in French dressings, pork roasts, poultry and fish.

*Thyme* - the leaves and stems of a shrub grown in France and Spain. It has a strong, distinctive flavor. Common Uses: for poultry season-ing, in croquettes, fricassees and fish dishes; also tasty on fresh sliced tomatoes.

*Turmeric* - a root of the ginger family, grown in India, Haiti, Jamaica and Peru. It is a mild, ginger-pepper flavor. Common Uses: as a fla-voring and coloring in prepared mustard and curries; also for meats, dressings, and salads.

## *ABBREVIATIONS*

| | |
|---|---|
| approx | approximately |
| doz | dozen |
| g | gram |
| lb | pound |
| mg | milligram |
| oz | ounce |
| pkg | package |
| qt | quart |
| Tbs | tablespoon |
| tsp | teaspoon |

## *EQUIVALENT MEASURES*

| | | |
|---|---|---|
| 3 tsp | = | 1 Tbs |
| 4 Tbs | = | 1/4 cup |
| 5 1/3 Tbs | = | 1/3 cup |
| 16 Tbs | = | 1 cup |
| 2 cups | = | 1 pint |
| 4 cups (2 pints) | = | 1 qt |
| 4 qts (liquid) | = | 1 gallon |

# INDEX

## A

Acorn Chops, 57

Apricot Chicken, 3

## B

Baby Carrots in Dilled
Sauce, 79

Baja Beef Strips, 36

Barbecued Beef, 32

Barbecued Turkey Legs, 46

Barley and Beef (low-fat), 76

Beef Barley Soup, 25

Beef Burgundy, insert

Beef Goulash, 33

Beef Short Ribs and
Potatoes, 43

Beef Stew, insert

Beef Stroganoff, 41

Beef Stroganoff, insert

Beef Tips with Onions and
Port, 27

Beefy Beans and Rice, 24

Beefy Mushrooms and
Potatoes (low-fat), 68

Blackeyed Peas and
Sausage, 59

Bok Choy Chicken, 19

Braised Leeks, 85

## C

Carnitas, 53

Castiglioni Stew, 30

Chicken Ala King, insert

Chicken and Dumplings, 11

Chicken and Eggplant
Parmesan, 9

Chicken and Tomatoes, 10

Chicken Cacciatore, insert

Chicken Corn Soup
(low-fat), 75

Chicken Creole, 20

Chicken Dijon, 6

Chicken Jambalaya, 17

Chicken Picante, 5

Chicken Satay, 12

Chicken Stew, 3

Chicken Tarragon, 10

Chicken Tetrazzini, 18

Chicken with Olives and
Capers, 4

Chicken with Sweet Red
Peppers, 20

Chicken with Vegetables,
insert

Corned Beef and Cabbage, 27

Corned Beef and
Vegetables, 39

Country Rosemary Chicken, 4

Creamy Potatoes (low-fat), 73

Creole Eggplant, 82

Crown Roast of Pork, 56

Curried Chicken (low-fat), 84

Curried Sweet Potatoes, 7

INDEX • *91*

# Notes

# Notes

# Notes

# Notes

# Notes

# Notes